Animals in My Yard

# Weasels

by Amy McDonald

BELLWETHER MEDIA
MINNEAPOLIS, MN

**Blastoff! Beginners** are developed by literacy experts and educators to meet the needs of early readers. These engaging informational texts support young children as they begin reading about their world. Through simple language and high frequency words paired with crisp, colorful photos, Blastoff! Beginners launch young readers into the universe of independent reading.

## Sight Words in This Book

| | | | |
|---|---|---|---|
| and | help | long | they |
| are | her | run | to |
| do | him | see | too |
| eat | I | their | white |
| for | in | them | you |
| have | jump | then | |

This edition first published in 2022 by Bellwether Media, Inc.

No part of this publication may be reproduced in whole or in part without written permission of the publisher. For information regarding permission, write to Bellwether Media, Inc., Attention: Permissions Department, 6012 Blue Circle Drive, Minnetonka, MN 55343.

Library of Congress Cataloging-in-Publication Data

Names: McDonald, Amy, author.
Title: Weasels / by Amy McDonald.
Description: Minneapolis, MN : Bellwether Media, 2022. | Series: Animals in my yard | Includes bibliographical references and index. | Audience: Ages 4-7 | Audience: Grades K-1
Identifiers: LCCN 2021040725 (print) | LCCN 2021040726 (ebook) | ISBN 9781644875643 (library binding) | ISBN 9781648345753 (ebook)
Subjects: LCSH: Weasels--Juvenile literature.
Classification: LCC QL737.C25 M3547 2022 (print) | LCC QL737.C25 (ebook) | DDC 599.76/62--dc23
LC record available at https://lccn.loc.gov/2021040725
LC ebook record available at https://lccn.loc.gov/2021040726

Text copyright © 2022 by Bellwether Media, Inc. BLASTOFF! BEGINNERS and associated logos are trademarks and/or registered trademarks of Bellwether Media, Inc.

Editor: Betsy Rathburn   Designer: Brittany McIntosh

Printed in the United States of America, North Mankato, MN.

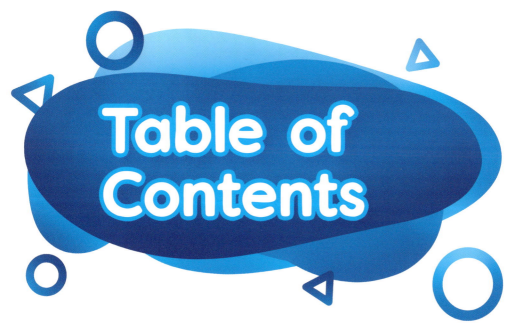

# Table of Contents

| | |
|---|---|
| Weasels! | 4 |
| Body Parts | 6 |
| The Lives of Weasels | 12 |
| Weasel Facts | 22 |
| Glossary | 23 |
| To Learn More | 24 |
| Index | 24 |

# Weasels!

Peek-a-boo!
I see you, weasel!

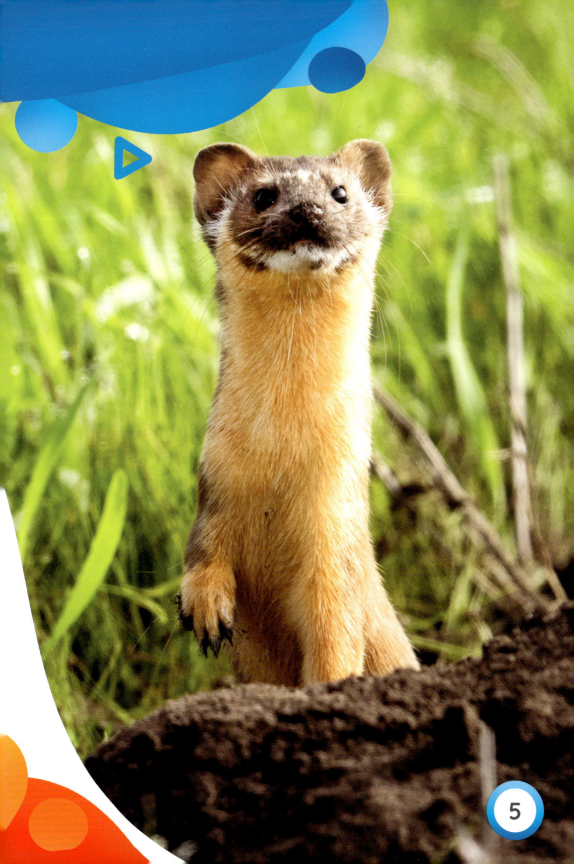

# Body Parts

Weasels have thick fur.
They turn white in snowy winters.

fur

They have long bodies. They have short legs.

They have sharp teeth. They bite **prey**.

teeth

prey

# The Lives of Weasels

Weasels hunt mice and frogs. They eat eggs, too!

mice

frogs

eggs

They smell food.
They run
and jump.
Then they bite!

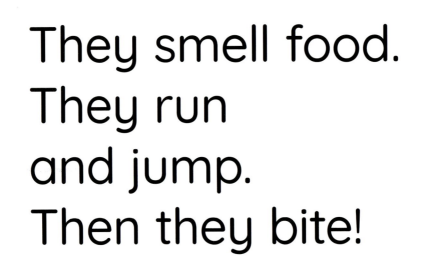

Mom brings food to her **kits**. Yum!

Weasels are food for owls and foxes. Snakes eat them, too!

fox

Their fur helps them hide.
Do you see him?

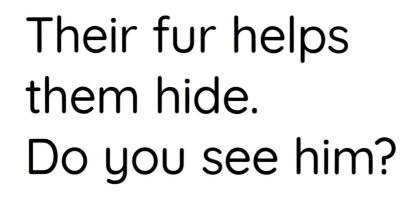

# Weasel Facts

## Weasel Body Parts

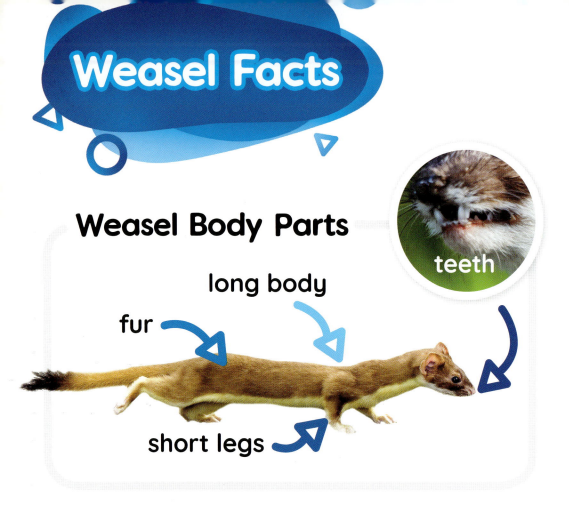

## Weasel Food

mice     frogs     eggs

# Glossary

**kits**

baby weasels

**prey**

animals that are food for other animals

# To Learn More

## ON THE WEB

# FACTSURFER

Factsurfer.com gives you a safe, fun way to find more information.

1. Go to www.factsurfer.com.

2. Enter "weasels" into the search box and click 🔍.

3. Select your book cover to see a list of related content.

# Index

| | | |
|---|---|---|
| bite, 10, 14 | jump, 14 | snakes, 18 |
| bodies, 8 | kits, 16, 17 | teeth, 10 |
| eggs, 12, 13 | legs, 8, 9 | white, 6 |
| food, 14, 16, 18 | mice, 12 | winters, 6 |
| foxes, 18 | mom, 16 | |
| frogs, 12, 13 | owls, 18 | |
| fur, 6, 20 | prey, 10, 11 | |
| hide, 20 | run, 14 | |
| hunt, 12 | smell, 14 | |

The images in this book are reproduced through the courtesy of: Wild Art, front cover, p. 6; Bokeholic, p. 3; Kelp Grizzly Photography, pp. 5, 15; Nicholas Taffs, p. 7; wildphoto3, p. 9; DV Wildlife/ Alamy, pp. 10 (teeth), 22 (teeth); Dolores M. Harvey, p. 11; jitkagold, pp. 12, 23 (prey); mavourneen strozewski/ Alamy, p. 13 (top); Karel Bock, pp. 13 (bottom left), 22 (mice); Anne Kitzman, p. 13 (bottom right); Nature Picture Library/ Alamy, p. 17; Eric Isselee, p. 18; Stephan Morris, p. 19; Frank Fichtmueller, p. 20; georgesanker/ Alamy, p. 21; All Canada Photos/ Alamy, p. 22; Ute Sonja Medley, p. 22 (frogs); Katelyn Dolson, p. 22 (eggs); Leo Bucher, p. 23 (kits).